MICHAEL JORDAN
BASKETBALL SUPERSTAR

Rob Kirkpatrick

To Elizabeth Geiser, the Michael Jordan of book publishing.

Published in 2001 by The Rosen Publishing Group, Inc.
29 East 21st Street, New York, NY 10010

First Edition

Book Design: Michael de Guzman

Photo Credits: p. 4 © Allsport; pp. 7, 15 © Jonathan Daniel/Allsport; p. 8 © Seth Poppel Yearbook Archives; p. 11 © Office of Sports Information, University of North Carolina and © AP Wide World; p. 12 © Jonathan Daniel/Allsport and © Ken Levine/Allsport; p. 16 © Craig Jones/Allsport; p. 19 © Vincent Laforet/Allsport and © Jonathan Daniel/Allsport; p. 20 © Andrew D. Bernstein, NBA Photos/Allsport; p. 22 © Reuters/Mike Blake/Archive Photos.

Kirkpatrick, Rob.
    Michael Jordan, basketball superstar / Rob Kirkpatrick.
      p. cm.— (Great record breakers in sports)
    Includes index.
    Summary: A brief biography of the basketball superstar, Michael Jordan, from his childhood in North Carolina through his career with the Chicago Bulls to his status as one of the sport's fifty greatest players.
    ISBN 0-8239-5633-4
    1. Jordan, Michael, 1963—Juvenile literature. 2. Basketball players—United States—Biography—Juvenile literature. [1. Jordan, Michael, 1963- 2. Basketball players. 3. Afro-Americans—Biography.] I. Title. II. Series.

GV884.J67 K57 2000
796.323'092—dc21
[B]   99-056857

Manufactured in the United States of America

CONTENTS

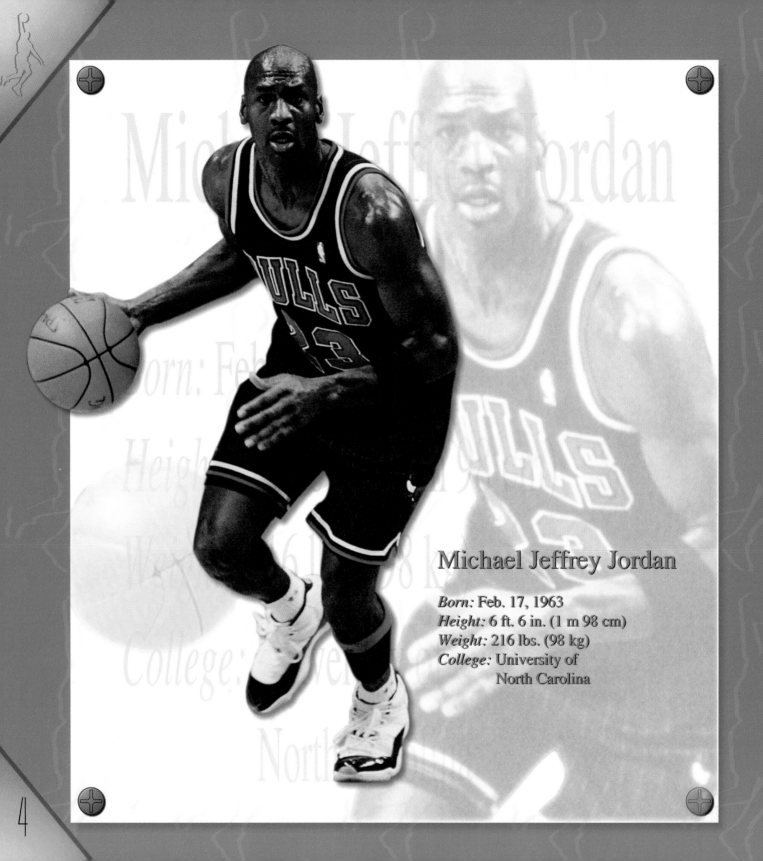

Michael Jeffrey Jordan

Born: Feb. 17, 1963
Height: 6 ft. 6 in. (1 m 98 cm)
Weight: 216 lbs. (98 kg)
College: University of
       North Carolina

MEET MICHAEL

Michael Jordan may be the most popular athlete on earth. He holds the **National Basketball Association**, or NBA, all-time **playoff** records for **points**, **scoring average**, and **steals**. He played a big part in helping his team, the Chicago Bulls, win six **championships** in the 1990s. Each time the Bulls won the NBA title, Michael was named the Most Valuable Player, or MVP, of the **finals**. The MVP is the award given to the best player in the NBA. His success in playoff games began before the Bulls were champions. On April 20, 1986, he set the record for the most points in one playoff game by scoring 63 points against the Boston Celtics!

◀ *Lots of people think Michael Jordan is the greatest basketball player in history.*

SETTING RECORDS

Records help us remember how players and teams have done in the past. They remind us of how great players were, even after they have stopped playing their sport. For example, some people may not have known who Wilt Chamberlain was. If you look at the NBA record book, you will see that on March 2, 1962, Wilt Chamberlain scored 100 points for the Philadelphia Warriors in a regular-season game against the New York Knicks! No one has ever scored more, not even Michael. People will remember Michael for a long time, too. He has set many records of his own.

Michael holds the NBA record for the highest career scoring average with his 31.5 points per game. ▶

MICHAEL'S RECORDS:

Highest Scoring Average - 31.5

Most Points in a Playoff Game - 63

Highest Scoring Average in Playoffs - 33.4

Most Points in Playoffs - 5,987

Most Steals in Playoffs - 376

HOOP DREAMS

Michael Jeffrey Jordan was born on February 17, 1963, in Brooklyn, New York. He and his family moved to Wilmington, North Carolina, when Michael was still young. Michael's father built a basketball court on the grass in the Jordan family's backyard. Michael played a lot of games on that grass court.

Michael tried out for his high school's **varsity** basketball team in the 10th grade. He did not make the team. Michael kept practicing and made the team the next year. In fact, he played so well in 12th grade that he earned a scholarship to play basketball with the University of North Carolina Tarheels.

◀ *When Michael was in the 12th grade, he led Wilmington's Laney High School basketball team to 19 wins.*

FROM NORTH CAROLINA TO CHICAGO

Michael was a great player in college. In his first year at the University of North Carolina, he hit the winning shot for the Tarheels in the national championship game. Michael was named the best player in college in both his **sophomore** and **junior** years. After his junior year in 1984, Michael decided to go **professional**. The Chicago Bulls drafted, or picked, him. Michael finished college in summer school over the next two years. The Bulls did not play well then, but Michael helped them make the playoffs in 1986. In one game against the Boston Celtics, Michael scored 63 points. No one has ever scored that many points in one playoff game.

In the last second of the 1982 championship game, Michael made a shot to win the game and the championship for the UNC Tarheels. ▶

Michael Jordan
was named college player
of the year in both his
sophomore and junior years.

– In a 1986 playoff game
against the Boston Celtics,
Michael Jordan scored 63 points.
This broke Elgin Baylor's 1962
record of 61 points.

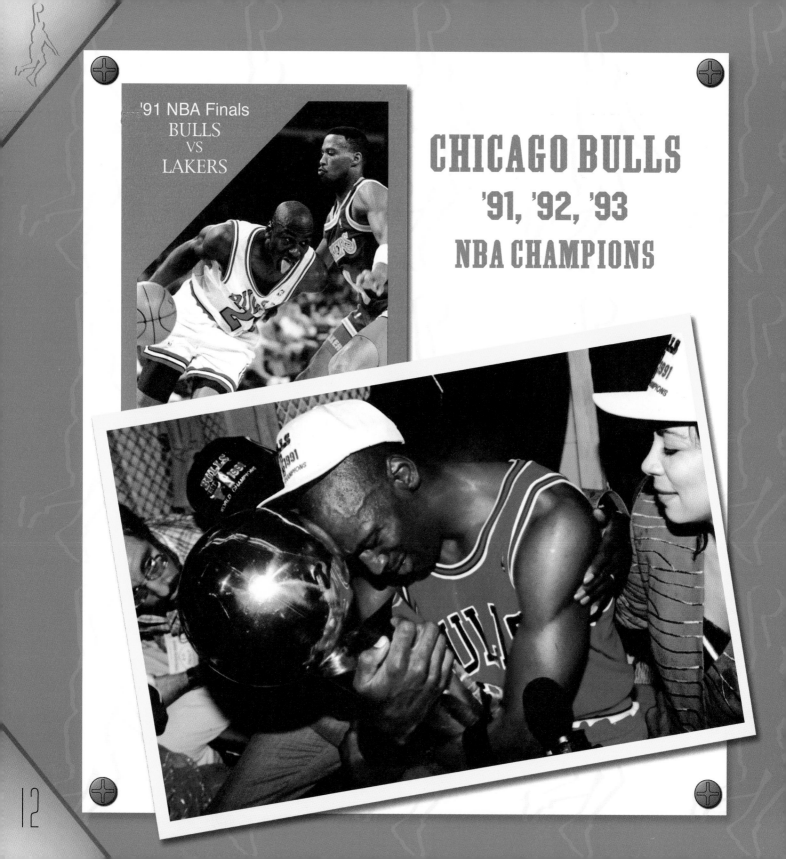

'91 NBA Finals
BULLS
VS
LAKERS

CHICAGO BULLS
'91, '92, '93
NBA CHAMPIONS

ON TOP OF THE WORLD

In 1986, the Bulls signed Michael to a new seven-year **contract**. In the contract, the Bulls agreed to pay him six million dollars for seven years. This made Michael the highest paid player in basketball. It was a lot of money, but it turned out to be a good decision for the Bulls. Michael and the Bulls got better and better. In 1991, they won their first national championship. One national championship was not enough. They went back to the finals and won again in 1992 and 1993. The Bulls were the best team in the NBA. Many people believed that Michael was the best basketball player in the whole world.

◄ *Michael won the MVP award in the NBA championship series for 1991, 1992, and 1993.*

A RECORD-SETTING SEASON

In 1993, Michael decided he wanted to play baseball instead of basketball. He was signed by the Chicago White Sox to play in their **minor league system**. He played in the outfield. Without Michael that year, the Bulls did not go to the finals. Michael did not play baseball as well as he had hoped. In 1995, he decided to play for the Bulls again. The 1995–96 season was his first full season back with the team, and it was a record-setting one. The Bulls won 72 games and lost only 10. As of 1999, this is the best single-season record ever.

Michael's team, the Chicago Bulls, set an NBA record in the 1995–96 season. The Bulls won 72 games and lost only 10. ▶

Most Regular-Season Wins

W -L	Team	Season
72-10	Chicago Bulls	1995-1996
69-13	L.A. Lakers	1971-1972
69-13	Chicago Bulls	1996-1997
68-13	Philadelphia 76ers	1966-1967
68-14	Boston Celtics	1972-1973
67-15	Boston Celtics	1985-1986
67-15	Chicago Bulls	1991-1992

Repeat
3peat

THREE MORE TITLES

The Bulls were champions again with Michael on their team. They liked having him back, so they gave him a new contract. They paid him 30 million dollars to play in the 1996–97 season. This was more money than anyone had ever been paid to play basketball. Michael came through for his team. He helped the Bulls win championships in 1997 and 1998. In the last game of the 1998 finals against the Utah Jazz, Michael made the game winning basket. He was named the finals MVP for the sixth time. This was another record.

◀ *Michael led the Bulls to six NBA championships.*

THE CHARGING BULLS

Michael was a great player for the Bulls, and he had a great team around him. Scottie Pippen, Dennis Rodman, Steve Kerr, and Toni Kukoc were some of the players who helped the Bulls become the best team in basketball. Their coach, Phil Jackson, also helped the team work together. Michael and the Bulls were so good that more and more people wanted to see them play. On March 27, 1998, in Atlanta, 62,046 fans came to see the Bulls play the Atlanta Hawks. That set a record for the highest attendance at one basketball game.

Coach Phil Jackson helped Michael and his Chicago teammates, like Scottie Pippen and Dennis Rodman, work well together. ▶

DENNIS RODMAN

SCOTTIE PIPPEN

PHIL JACKSON

MICHAEL JORDAN

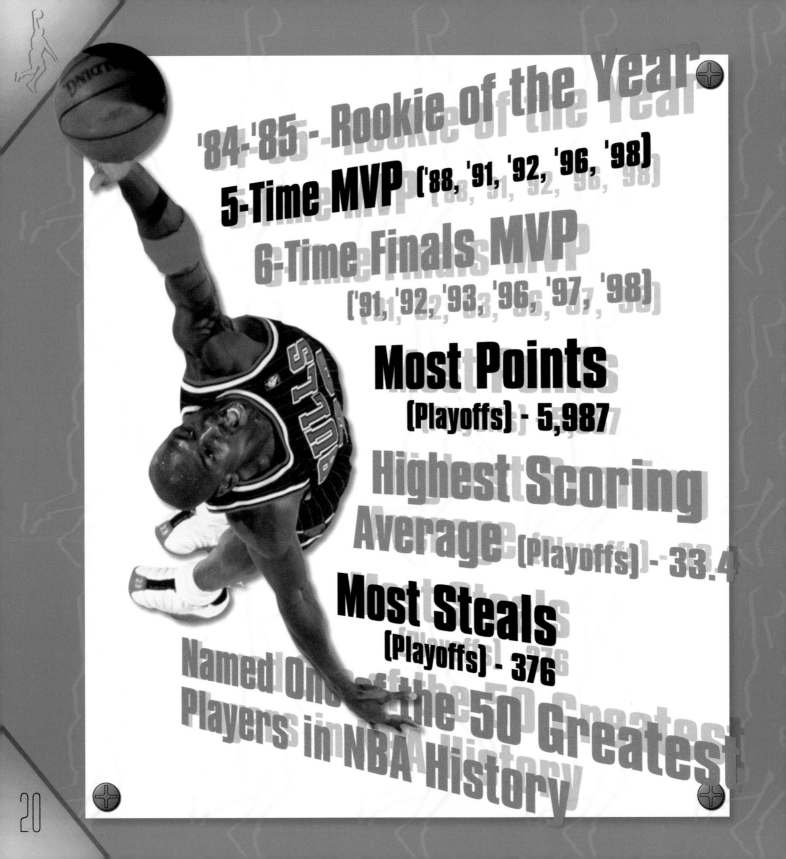

MICHAEL RETIRES ON TOP

After the 1997–98 season, Michael decided he did not want to play in the NBA anymore. He retired from professional basketball. He had an amazing career from beginning to end. He is one of only 12 players to win both the Rookie of the Year award, which is given to the best first-year player in the NBA, and the MVP. He was named one of the 50 greatest players in NBA history. His 5,987 points, 376 steals, and 33.4 scoring average are playoff records. He also holds the all-time regular-season scoring average record of 31.5 points per game.

◀ *With his record-breaking skills and love for the sport, Michael has helped make basketball popular around the world.*

A LIVING LEGEND

Michael is one of the greatest record breakers of all time. He and his number 23 jersey, or sports shirt, became so famous because of his success on the basketball court that he is recognized wherever he goes. He has done many commercials for products he likes, and he even starred in his own movie, *Space Jam*.

Michael's fans will never forget him. Young NBA players still remember him. For many years to come, new players will join the NBA and try to "be like Mike."

GLOSSARY

championships (CHAM-pee-un-ships) The last games of a sports season that decide which team is the best.

contract (KAHN-trakt) A signed agreement between a player and a team.

finals (FY-nuhls) A series of games played by the two best teams in the playoffs. The winning team is the national champion.

junior (JOO-nyor) A student's third year in high school or college.

minor league system (MY-nor LEEG SIS-tem) A group of teams with players who are trying to make the major league baseball teams.

National Basketball Association (NBA) (NAH-shuh-nul BAS-kit-bol uh-SOH-see-AY-shun) A league, or group, of the best professional basketball teams in North America.

playoff (PLAY-off) A game played at the end of the season by the best teams. The team that wins the most playoff games wins the NBA championship.

points (POYNTS) Units of scoring.

professional (pro-FEH-shuh-nul) An athlete who earns money for playing a sport.

scoring average (SKOR-ing AV-er-ehj) A player's total points divided by the number of games he has played.

sophomore (SAHF-mor) A student's second year of high school or college.

steals (STEELZ) When a player takes the basketball from the other team.

varsity (VAR-sih-tee) The main team in a high school sport.

INDEX

A
Atlanta Hawks, 18

B
Boston Celtics, 5, 10

C
Chamberlain, Wilt, 6
championships, 5, 10, 13, 17
Chicago Bulls, 5, 10, 13, 14, 17, 18
Chicago White Sox, 14

J
Jackson, Phil, 18

K
Kerr, Steve, 18
Kukoc, Toni, 18

M
MVP, 5, 17, 21

N
New York Knicks, 6
North Carolina Tarheels, 9, 10

P
Philadelphia Warriors, 6
Pippen, Scottie, 18
playoffs, 5, 10, 21

points, 5, 10, 21

R
records, 5, 6, 14, 17, 18, 21, 22
Rodman, Dennis, 18

S
scoring average, 5, 21
Space Jam, 22
steals, 5, 21

U
Utah Jazz, 17

WEB SITES

To learn more about Michael Jordan, check out these Web sites:

http://www.nba.com/bulls
http://jordan.sportsline.com
http://wwwnba.com/playerfile/michael_jordan.html